**CORNWALL COUNTY COUNCIL
LIBRARIES AND ARTS DEPARTMENT**

ONE AND ALL

FAL	
HEL	
PEN	
PER	
SAG	
TRU	7/98

CORNWALL'S CHURCHYARD HERITAGE

Hilary Lees

St Petroc's Church, Padstow

GOD'S ACRE

TO WALK THROUGH an ancient churchyard s to step back into history; to absorb something of a place that has been sacred for hundreds, perhaps thousands of years. To run your finger over carved angels' wings and decipher age-old names under sunken, lichen-covered stones. Every churchyard is a legacy to the skills of our ancestors, a reflection of contemporary life with its frailties and tragedies and a mine of information to archaeologists and historians. But most of all it is a place for rest and reflection among old friends, a haven for wildlife; a place very much for the living as well as the dead.

For most people, the church is the physical and spiritual centre of a community. A pinnacled mediaeval tower, a distant spire glimpsed between tall trees, is enough to say that here is a place, a community, a collection of people who live together in this town or village.

The God's Acre on which the church stands may have been a site of religious significance for hundreds of years longer than the church which now stands on it. The churchyard is the setting for the church and part of its history; it lends character and proportion to the building, enabling one to stand back and look at the church in the context of its surroundings. It is also the hallowed ground in which rest the remains of its worshippers and workers from generations past.

The memorials in the churchyards of Cornwall are a monument, literally, to the art of the letter-cutter and the sculptor. They tell us something of the people who worked and worshipped here: sailors, master mariners, wives, children, servants, friends. Of how and when they died and who grieved for them. Many have epitaphs: moral, sentimental, humorous, or enigmatic, a whole art form of its own.

In Cornwall the slate from which most of the memorials are carved has weathered well, and many of the carvings are as sharp after two hundred years as the day they were cut. The development from the crude early styles to the highly ornate forms of the nineteenth century and the simple dignity of modern work can be seen in churchyards all over the county; Padstow, St Minver, St Endellion, Saltash, all have interesting collections spanning three hundred years.

Each churchyard has a character of its own; some are neglected and overgrown, the memorials crumbling and dangerous, eaten into by ivy and years of weathering. Others are overmown, the grass as neat as a bowling green, the headstones moved to the boundary to make way for the all-consuming mower. In recent years the value of churchyards as conservation areas has become increasingly recognised. Many of them are undisturbed original meadowland; they may be home to rare plants and insects, lichens and mosses. They are a haven for birds and animals at a time when the farmland that used to surround our village churches has become increasingly barren.

Sir John Betjeman, much loved poet of Cornwall, who himself lies under a superb modern stone at St Enodoc, obviously had a great affection for churchyards everywhere:

> For churchyards then, though hallowed ground
> Were not so grim as now they sound,
> And horns of ale were handed round
> For which churchwardens used to pay
> On each especial vestry day.

> 'Twas thus the village drunk its beer
> With its relations buried near,
> And that is why we often see
> Inns where the alehouse used to be
> Close to the church where prayers were said
> And Masses for the village dead.

> But this I know, you're sure to find
> Some headstones of the Georgian kind
> In each old churchyard near and far,
> Just go and see how fine they are.
> Notice the lettering of that age
> Spaced like a noble title-page,
> The parish names cut deep and strong
> To hold the shades of evening long,
> The quaint and sometimes touching rhymes
> By parish poets of the times,
> Bellows, or reaping hook or spade
> To show perhaps the dead man's trade,
> And cherubs in the corner spaces
> With wings and English ploughboy faces ...
> CHURCHYARDS

THE HISTORY OF THE CHURCHYARD

Since prehistoric times, long before the arrival of Christianity, the burial of the dead and the rituals associated with it were taking place. Cornwall is rich in prehistoric monuments: standing stones, circles, quoits and barrows which would all have had a religious - albeit pagan - significance. A tomb was considered simply to be a house for the dead, and the grave goods which were buried with the corpse indicated a belief in some form of after-life.

The earliest settled farmers of the late Neolithic and early Bronze Age periods buried their dead in communal chambered tombs constructed from enormous slabs of granite such as Lanyon Quoit and Trevethy Quoit. The chamber tombs found on Scilly and known as entrance graves are a variant of the chambered tomb.

Standing stones, or menhirs were probably way markers or boundary stones, and the burials occasionally found near them may

suggest that some were memorial stones or grave markers. Bronze Age barrows or prominent sites, where excavation has revealed grave goods such as jewellery and daggers, were probably the graves o prominent people.

From the early Iron Age burials were in pit graves, with the bodies placed on their sides in a crouched position on a north-south alignment. In 1900 a cemetery of stone cist (box) graves was found at Harlyn Bay, near S Merryn with grave goods of Mediterranean origin.

Throughout the Roman occupation Cornwall seems to have remained essentially Celtic in character. With only one Roman fort partially excavated, the minimal excursions into Cornwall have left no trace of Roman burials although a Roman altar was found on S Mary's during the last century. After the withdrawal of the Romans, the developing Christian church was the one unifying facto among the small communities of Cornwall. The tireless band of missionaries and priests are remembered in the unusual dedications of our churches, although little is known about many of them: St Pinnock, St Veep, St Winnow, St Winwallo and hundreds more.

At Tintagel archaelogists have found the ruins of an pre-Norman stone church and have been able to trace the history of mediaeval burial practices over hundreds of years. When Pope Gregory I sent St Augustine to convert the British he shrewdly specified that the pagan temples were to be converted to the new religion, thus allowing continuity of worship in one place. It seems likely that many of the holy wells were also pagan in origin, as the tradition of water having supernatural powers dates from Pre-Christian times.

Many modern churches now stand on sites that are of pagan origin; the best indication is to be found in the remains of earth-banked enclosures known 'lan', a prefix which among modern place-names indicates an early Christian site. Churchyards that are circular, such as St Buryan, Lanivet and St Mabyn, are likely to have been early Christian enclosed settlements, perhaps even monastic communities containing a chapel and a burial ground. Priests travelled out from these monastic houses to preach, to celebrate mass and to baptise the converts to the new faith. A cross would have been erected and a makeshift altar built in front of it until such time as a more permanent one was made and enclosed in a primitive hut. It was a small step to building some sort of shelter for themselves, and so the first church buildings were born.

As the Christian message spread, so daughter churches were built in the centres of population, and wealthy landowners had churches built on their own land; Lanhydrock and Mawgan-in-Pydar are good examples of churches which stand in the lee of a manor house.

By the fifth and sixth centuries Christianity was becoming well established from Ireland and Wales. In 752 AD St Cuthbert was granted permission by the Pope to establish churchyards around churches, marking out the cardinal points with crosses. The purpose was to ensure that Masses were said for the dead to speed the passage of their souls through Purgatory, and that the living were reminded of their own mortality.

In the tenth century the practice of enclosing one acre was introduced, the origin of the term God's Acre. Pagan rituals and beliefs were still not far below the surface, and the tradition of the churchyard being a place of sanctuary dates from earliest times.

The mediaeval churchyard was the centre of village life in much the same way as the village hall of today. Fairs and markets were held, travelling pedlars sold their wares; musicians played, competitions in archery and other sports were held, livestock were bought and sold. 'Church Ales' were held on feast days to raise money for the poor and for the upkeep of the church, and to augment the priest's income. The porch was considered to be the place for serious business, for taking oaths and settling disputes; many church porches still have an image niche in front of which solemn vows would be sworn.

At first only priests were buried inside the church; the vast majority of the population were buried in the churchyard in simple shrouds, without a coffin. The body would be laid on its back facing east on an east/west alignment, another relic of pagan worship of the sun-god. Burials would start at one end of the churchyard and when the burial ground was full they would go back to the beginning and start again. Eventually there would be two or more layers of bones in very shallow graves, and it became necessary to remove some of them to the crypt or charnel house in the church. In several ancient churchyards there is such an accumulation of bodies that the surface of the ground has been raised several feet, and a channel has had to be cut around the church for drainage purposes. Kenneth Lindley calculated in 'Of Graves and Epitaphs' that a twelfth-century churchyard with only six burials a year would by now contain some 4,800 bodies. At Lanhydrock there is a long row of unmarked graves beside the path; no-one knows who is buried there; they are a salutary reminder to us all of the ultimate anonymity of death. The area to the south of the church is where the oldest graves are to be found; the choice of the sunny side may reflect the pagan worship of the sun-god. The north side, in the shadow of the church, was reserved for suicides, criminals, strangers and unbaptised babies. There were no churchyard memorials: anyone rich or important enough to have a monument erected would be buried inside the church.. On the outside wall of the church at Linkinhorne is a stone commemorating the deaths of Catherine Nicholls and Joan Mullins who died in 1742 and 1744 respectively. The stone is carved with a skeleton, an arrow and a spade, and is signed by Daniel Gumb, an eccentric mason who lived with his wife and children in a lonely cottage near the Cheesewring and died in 1776. The neat little epitaph records the feelings of those buried outside:

Railed chest tomb at Lanteglos-by-Camelford

Here we lye without the wall
Twas full within they made a brawl.
Here we lye no rent to pay
And yet we lye so warm as they.

The nineteenth century and the Industrial Revolution saw a migration of population into urban centres which created problems of overcrowding for city churchyards. Grave robbing became a profitable business with as much as £20 being paid by medical schools for a 'good clean corpse' as improvements in surgical techniques created a demand for bodies for dissection. Heavy ledger stones were placed over new graves as a deterrent to body snatchers; the fashion for iron railings was part of the Victorian perspective on the the privacy of the dead.

As city churchyards became increasingly foul and unhygienic the Burial Act of 1852 was passed to allow cemeteries to be set up by local authorities in the same way as drainage and water services. To this day cemeteries have little of the character of churchyards; regimented rows of cheap imported marble are the result of improvements in transport and the rise of the monumental mason, and have nothing of the appeal of local stone or slate. Cremation, which only became legal as recently as 1884, has brought a new element to our churchyards: small cremation plaques which line the path or form a Garden of Remembrance.

In our own century we have a small reminder of ancient customs: while interments still take place with the head facing the east, a priest is still brought into his own funeral service 'versus altare' with his head to the west,: facing the congregation, and is then buried facing in the same direction.

St Levan's stone

It is sometimes said of Cornwall that it is not the architecture itself, but the setting of the architecture that makes an impression. From the rocky cliffs of the north to the wooded valleys of the south, the solid, rough-hewn church outlines reflect the durability and austerity of the Cornish way of life. Often the anticipation is as exciting as the arrival: the green-tunnelled lanes to Lanteglos-by-Fowey; the walk to Grade, or Advent, churches almost in a field; or the clifftop churches like St Genny's, Talland or Morwenstow, with the sea spread out at your feet. And always there is the reminder of Cornwall's close relationship with the sea: Rock, where the tide washes against the churchyard wall; St Winnow, at the river's edge, and the sand-locked church at Gunwalloe where the separate tower looks out stolidly over the bay. Sometimes it is not only the churchyard itself but the outlook that

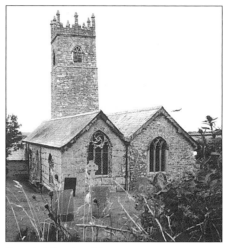

Pinnacled church at Advent

is captivating: St Dennis, which is built inside an Iron Age hillfort 700 feet up, above the extraordinary scenery of the china clay workings. Redruth, which looks out over the remains of the tin-mining industry, and where the pinnacled lych gate has a coffin stone large enough to accommodate three coffins, because of the number of mining disasters in the area.

And then there is Minster, with its woodland churchyard, set so deep in its valley that you can drive past it and not know it's there; the shears on the outside of the tower a reminder that this was once sheep country.

Hidden church of Minster

Mounting block, Sancreed

LYCH GATES AND BOUNDARIES

The main entrance to a large number of Cornish churchyards is through a lych gate, many of which still have coffin stones. The name is derived from the Anglo-Saxon word lich meaning corpse; the purpose of the roofed lych gate was for the bearers to shelter and to rest the coffin as they waited for the priest, who was required by the Prayer Book of 1549 to meet the coffin at the entrance to the churchyard and there begin the service. Often there are also seats for the bearers, and some lych gates also have 'Cornish stiles' or cattle grids, spaced stone slabs to stop cattle wandering into the churchyard. At St Just-in-Roseland there are two lych gates with slate seats, the upper one with what must be the best church view in Cornwall, the lower one

Lych gate with coffin stone, Kilkhampton

Slate-hung upper room, Kenwyn

with a cattle grid. At Little Petherick there is a coffin stone but no lych gate, which may indicate that at the time the small parish could not afford the roofed structure.

Another feature more common in Cornwall than elsewhere is the lych gate with a room above. Feock, Kenwyn and St Clement have slate-hung upper rooms, while the seventeenth century lych gate at Wendron has a granite-built parish room. A number of churchyards have buildings as part of the boundary: at Phillack the old prison forms part of the churchyard wall, built in great black blocks of copper slag. St Hilary and St Mewan both have ancient buildings; St Teath has a parish room which is still in use; Madron has a schoolroom whose founder lies in the churchyard nearby. Most attractive of all is the buttressed fourteenth century guildhouse at Poundstock, built of cob and stone and with

Parish room, Wendron

Wrought iron gates, Padstow

stiles at Grade, St Levan, St Anthony-in-Meneage and many more. At Lanhydrock the church stands in the shadow of the house, which itself forms part of the boundary.

Usually just outside the churchyard gates there may be a mounting block, a reminder of the days when the congregation came to church on horseback. The enchanting Quaker burial ground at Come-To-Good has not only a mounting block inside the gates, but stables as well for the comfort of the horses during services. Altarnun, Sancreed and St Buryan also have mounting blocks and in several churchyards they are incorporated into the wall, like the one at Jacobstow.

wooden mullions. The sloping churchyard, the old building, the lych gate and the stream that runs alongside make one of the most picturesque settings in the county.

Sometimes a stile allows pedestrians into the churchyard while keeping cattle out, like the great slab at Morwenstow. There are also slate

14th century Guildhouse, Poundstock

The outside of the church is also very much part of the churchyard, in particular the ornamented tower walls at St Austell and Fowey and the highly decorated exterior at Launceston. Probus, with the highest tower in Cornwall is certainly the most magnificent, with bands of carving demonstrating the astonishing skills of the mediaeval builders and craftsmen. Sometimes it is the architecture of the building itself that is unusual, like the remarkable west end of the church at Quethiock, or the strange tower at Lostwithiel. At Golant, a peaceful churchyard above the River Fowey, there is a holy well in the corner between the tower and the porch, and at Lewannick the decorated west door and the window above with its ogee hood and finials are a pleasant change from the usual Cornish austerity.

The early mediaeval carvings of grotesques and gargoyles, of fearsome beasts and crude figures, demonstrate the continuing belief, of pagan origin, in the conflict between the forces of good and evil. On the outside of the Colshull chapel at Duloe are animals which look like monkeys leering down from the parapet; on the tall, proud tower at Lanlivery angels and beasts form the corbel table at the top of the second stage. Grotesques and gargoyles lean out from the top stage of the tower at Breage, and at Cury the west door has heads as label stops which have watched

Sundial 1735, Advent

the passing congregation for five hundred years, their mouths open in permanent surprise. The tower parapet at South Hill is supported by twelve apostles, and at St Dominic there are three curious little figures in a recessed panel on each side.

Occasionally odd figures are found at the entrance to the church: Veryan has a single corbel above the west door and an unusual

hears on the tower, Minster

Corbel head, Veryan

capital with six heads on the left-hand jamb. At Egloshayle snakes decorate the west doorway, and at Treneglos two lions face each other across the tympanum. Crantock and Forrabury have fish weathervanes, while St Dennis has a ship in full sail, both reminders of Cornwall's traditional crafts.

A number of churches have slate sundials, many of them eighteenth century and most attractively carved, and often signed and with a motto, like the one at Wenn which has a pun: Ye Know Not When. They are usually, but not always, on the porch. In particularly fine condition are those at Advent, Blisland, Botus Fleming, Lansallos, Lelant, Paul, and St Levan. Luxulyan and Mawgan-in-Meneage have pillar sundials.

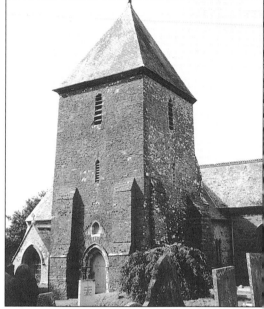

Leaning tower, Duloe

IN THE GROUNDS

The churchyard itself can contain a great deal of interest apart from the memorials, and sometimes a few surprises. Cornwall has several separate towers, at Feock, Gunwalloe, Gwennap, Illogan, Lamorran and Talland, where the churchyard hangs over the bay and a seat has thoughtfully been provided. In the churchyard at Bodmin is the ruined chapel of Sir Thomas Becket, and the quaint mediaeval structure called St Germoe's chair occupies the corner of the churchyard at Germoe.

St Germoe's Chair

No-one visiting Cornwall can fail to notice that nearly every churchyard has at least one cross, and many have several. In fact Cornwall has the largest and most varied number of crosses - over three hundred - of any county in the British Isles. Many of these may have been ancient stones of pre-Christian significance, re-used and carved for the new faith. They can be found on the moors, by the roadside, built into walls and buildings and most of all in churchyards. Wayside crosses would have marked pilgrim routes in the days when Cornwall was a bleak and barren place. They would also have marked sacred sites and commemorated the dead. There is an old tradition which says that richer pilgrims used to leave alms on the wayside crosses for the poorer brethren who followed them. In later years many stones, such as those at Zennor, marked the route for burial processions. In 1447 the rector of Creed left a bequest so that stone crosses could be erected 'where dead bodies are rested on their way to burial, that prayers may be made and the bearers take some rest.'

With the single exception of St Breage, where the churchyard cross is sandstone, all inscribed stones and crosses are made of granite, a material which does not lend itself to delicate

Pillar stone with Saxon inscription,
Lanteglos-by-Camelford

Wheelhead cross, Mawgan-in-Pydar

XP stone, Phillack

carving. Yet their solidity and rough texture is reassuring to the eye, representing as they do a continuity of faith which far outlives the present church by which they stand. A considerable number of churchyard crosses have only re-emerged relatively recently, having been lost, as at Cury, where the cross was rescued from a ditch, or buried as at Wendron, which has one of the oldest. Often they have been built into the fabric of the churchyard walls or the church itself. It may be that with the disappearance of the Celtic church they ceased to have a religious significance and were discarded, or they may have been hidden for protection at the Reformation.

The earliest form of Christian monuments are not crosses, but inscribed stones, the oldest of

Inscribed cross with figure of Christ, Sancreed

Cross shaft with interlace ornament, St Neot

which date from the late fifth century and bear the Chi Rho monogram, made up of the letters XP, the first two letters of the Greek word for Christ. The monogram was known to have been in use in Gaul until the end of the fifth century when it later developed into the figure of the cross as the symbol of Christ. Of those surviving in Cornwall one on the gable of the porch at Phillack, the others inside the churches at St Just-in-Penwith and at Lanteglos-by-Fowey. Inscribed stones, dating from the fifth to seventh centuries commemorated important people and can be found at Phillack and St Hilary. In the churchyard at Lewannick (with another inside the church) is a stone inscribed with Oghan lettering which can be fairly accurately dated to the late fifth or early sixth century. It is

6th century cross head at Wendron

Early cross with projections.
Lanteglos-by-Camelford

Four-holed cross with figure of Christ, Phillack

curious script which originated in southern Ireland and is made up of unconnected vertical strokes. There are other Ogham stones at St Clement and St Kew. At Lanivet a pillar stone now in the church is inscribed with the word ANNICU in Roman capitals. Other pillar stones are at Gulval, Lanteglos-by-Camelford and South Hill.

Crosses are generally more numerous in the west of the county, with wheelhead crosses by far the most common. They are usually of the type known as Celtic, with square arms linked by a circular ring. Giving a date to early crosses is difficult, as they have no architectural mouldings. Wheelhead crosses are by far the most numerous, with variations in the shape of the head and with the form of the cross which is carved in relief. There are good examples of plain wheelhead crosses in almost every churchyard, but among the best are those at Altarnun, Gunwalloe, St Juliot, St Levan (on the churchyard wall), Luxulyan and St Mabyn. Wheelhead crosses with the figure of Christ are at Feock, Sancreed and Zennor.

Crosses that are pierced between the

Cross at Quethiock, second highest in Cornwall

sculpture, such as those at Phillack and Sancreed, dates from the tenth century and later. The earliest form of decoration was an incised cross or design as at Cury and the one north of the church at Lanivet. The cross at St Levan also has a figure of Christ and is said by Langdon to be the 'most elegant and well-proportioned.' He also described the beautiful cross shaft with interlace ornament at St Neot as 'the best example of interlaced work in Cornwall.'

Four-holed ornamented crosses are found at St Columb Major, Lanhydrock, St Minver, Lanivet and Quethiock, at over thirteen feet one of the tallest. The four-holed cross at Mylor is perhaps the oldest Celtic cross in England, and with seven feet of its length in the ground it is certainly the tallest. The cross at Cardinham is said to be the finest in the country.

Later crosses date from the mediaeval period; there is a lantern cross at Mawgan-in-Pydar and others at Lostwithiel, Lanteglos-by-Fowey and Callington.

Mediæval lantern cross, Lostwithiel

projections of the arms are known as holed crosses, nearly all with four holes. Plain four-holed crosses can be seen at St Buryan, St Erth, Michaelstow, Paul and Wendron,

From the eighth to the twelfth century the figure of Christ was shown alive, dressed in a tunic, the limbs extended along three arms of the cross, the head erect on the fourth. Arthur G Langdon in his definitive book Old Cornish Crosses describes the representations of Christ as 'of the rudest and most grotesque description, being executed in low relief, rarely projecting more than an inch.'

Carved crosses are easier to date, as other documents of the period contain similar ornament. The widespread use of carved crosses with Celtic decoration or figure

MEMORIALS

Churchyard memorials come in all shapes and sizes, from the strictly functional to the ostentatious or even bizarre. In Cornwall the vast majority are slate headstones, a natural progression from the carved monoliths of the pre-Christian era. Their simple, satisfactory shapes do exactly what they are meant to do: commemorate the deceased and mark the place where they are buried. Every churchyard will have dozens: they are an important part of the history of the parish, often recording the status of the humbler members of the community. They record who lived here, when and often how they died. They reflect changes in social history such as the appalling levels of child mortality, and they demonstrate the development of the skill of the slate carver over two hundred years.

The earliest surviving memorials are the coped stones or hogbacks, which date from the Anglo-Norman period. The one at Lanivet has a key pattern with knotwork, and dog-like creatures on the ends. There is another at St Tudy, now inside the church, and incomplete ones at Phillack and St Buryan.

Churchyards as we know them today are post-Reformation. The oldest slate memorials are

Skull and crossbones, Botus Fleming

the enchanting horizontal slate memorial slabs, or ledgers of the sixteenth and seventeenth centuries which would once have covered chest tombs. The majority that survive are now inside the church; they are carved in relief, the inscriptions incised. There are beautiful examples at Poundstock, Rock, St Eval, and many more. At St Merryn they have been set into the ground outside the east end of the church; at Padstow there is one on the churchyard wall with an allegorical epitaph, and at Grade the ledger

Coped stone, Lanivet

Gruesome skull, Veryan

to Hugh Mason, who died in 1671, is on the outside north wall of the chancel. Alice Bizley, in her book The Slate Figures of Cornwall, thinks this may have been the first burial on the north side of the church, which would account for the tone of the epitaph:

Why here? Why not? 'tis all one ground
And here none will my dust confound.
My Saviour lay where no one did;
Why not a member as his head?
No quire to sing, no bells to ring?
Why, Sirs, thus buried was my King!
I grudge the fashion of this day,
To fat the church and starve the lay:
Though nothing now of me be seene
I hope my name and bed is greene.

On the outside wall of the porch at Callington is a memorial to Ann Holliday who died in 1753. It is carved in a fine-textured slate which is well preserved, and has all the symbolism of the period: angels blowing trumpets, and Christ trampling on the skeleton of Death. It is signed by John Burt.

Perhaps the most engaging of them all is the memorial to John Mably and his daughter Alice at St Enodoc, which is now in the porch and has stone portraits of them both. Cast iron crosses are not common, although there are several at St Erth. At Little Petherick is one dated 1895 which has no name; it says simply: Born, baptised, died in a day.

Memorial in a field, Botus Fleming

CHEST TOMBS

Chest tombs, sometimes called table tombs, are the outdoor equivalent of the altar tomb inside the church. Strictly speaking, table tombs have a leg at each corner supporting the ledger; we only saw one in Cornwall and that was at Gunwalloe. Both developed from the need to raise the ledgers above the

Headstone 1752, St Just-in-Roseland

Sarcophagus with finial, St Erth

encroaching vegetation; they are hollow, built of brick, slate or granite with the ledger on top. One of the earliest is the tomb dated 1609 at Davidstow to Peter Nelayer. Another at Linkinhorne is a memorial to John Binnick who died the eight and 20 (sic) day of November 1684. It has a skull like a child's drawing and a long inscription with strange spelling, largely

indecipherable. It begins:
Here underneath this stone lyes his corps ...
At Warbstow there is a pleasing collection of ten slate chest tombs from 1735 to 1826 to the Gillard and Grigg families, the ledgers decorated with angels and classical lettering. There is a set of three granite chest tombs to the Blight family at Stoke Climsland, and three panelled slate tombs with pilasters to the Gobeldick family at Mawgan-in-Pydar dated 1843.

TOMBS ECCENTRIC AND UNUSUAL

In every county there are monuments which do not fall into conventional categories. Cornwall has one which is not even in a churchyard; in the corner of a field some distance from the church at Botus Fleming is an obelisk to William Martyn who, being 'a Catholic Christian, in the true, not depraved Popish sense of the word,' had 'no superstitious veneration for church or churchyard' and preferred to be buried in unconsecrated ground. The obelisk is twelve feet tall, surrounded by a decrepit wrought-iron fence and overwhelmed by brambles. It is some distance from the road, and because of the bull in the field we risked life and limb to

Slate chest tombs, Warbstow

find it.
There are mausolea at
Madron, Treslothan and
Veryan. A structure shaped
like a nissan hut in the
churchyard at Ruan
Lanihorne covers the
entrance to a vault and is
known as Lukes' Tomb.
One of the oddest
memorials is the wooden
figure of Willaim Tinney at
Crantock, the last man to
be held in the stocks, 'a
smuggler and a vagabond.'
He sits with his arms
crossed, a feather in his
jaunty hat, his bootless feet in the stocks. The
story is told of how he 'robbed a widow
woman with violence' and was placed in the
stocks to await justice. He managed to escape
and 'in the sympathetic view of certain village
worthies bolted, got off to sea and was never
brought to justice or seen in the
neighbourhood again.'

Hawkins monument, Probus

But perhaps most splendid of all is the tomb to
Sir Christopher Hawkins, 1829, in Probus
churchyard. It has four almost life-size kneeling
figures in armour supporting the upper corners
of the tomb, which is decorated with
ornamented pilasters, angel heads and
elaborately framed cartouches.

Panelled slate chest tombs, St Mawgan-in-Pydar

Attractive lettering and angels 1763, Week St Mary

Detailed carving 1784, Lelant

The durability of Cornish slate has one great advantage: it wears so well that it enables us to examine the complete history of post-Reformation letter-forms over more than two hundred years.

The early stone masons were not specialists; they were what would nowadays be called jobbing builders who undertook memorial carving as a sideline. Large families and a high infant mortality rate ensured that there was no shortage of work for the village mason.

The seventeenth century ledgers already described are carved in relief with the inscriptions inscised. The lettering is simple with archaic, erratic spelling. Few headstones survive from then; in the eighteenth century relief carving was almost entirely abandoned and engraved designs had taken over. Designs at this stage had not reached the sophistication of other areas, a reflection of Cornwall's geographical isolation. There was little attention to layout: lettering was poorly spaced, with words often split or carried over into the margin.

By the middle of the eighteenth century the effects of the growth of printing and typesetting was beginning to be felt. As writing with a pen became a desirable skill writing masters produced 'copy-books' which were engraved on copper plates for printing, the origin of what became known as copper-plate handwriting. Copy-books provided slate and

Attractive layout 1843, Calstock

Decoration of the word in the 'head' 1849, Launcells

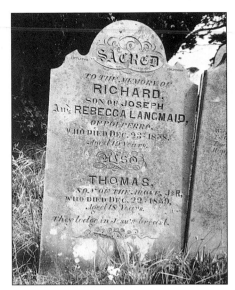

Headstone with signature 1838, Talland

stone carvers with a whole new range of letter styles and architectural designs, many of which can be seen on Cornish tombstones. The charming Cornish angels that occupy the head

Shadow lettering and decorated border 1870, St Endellion

of the stone with their variety of expressions and hairstyles are a direct result of the calligraphic influence.

Burgess recalls a Cornish tombstone-engraver called William Westaway who was the village schoolmaster at Bradworthy, just over the Devon border. He was renowned for his copper-plate handwriting and used to work at his tombstones while teaching.

Towards the end of the century the rapid spread of printing and typefounding meant that cheap illustrated copy-books were in common circulation; finely cut flowing italics and ornate capitals replaced the heavier relief of the previous century. Frequently the word at the head of the stone, such as 'In' or 'Memory' was

St Mabyn 1872

highly decorated. Letter-cutting was recognised as a true art form, and masons signed their names with a flourish, sometimes calling themselves Sculptor. The copy-books also brought architectural designs such as Adam-style draped urns, classical weeping figures and drooping foliage.

By the early nineteenth century a number of experimental typefaces

Copy-book stone 1874, Blisland

Machine cut lettering 1853, Germoe

were introduced and were rapidly copied by the slate-cutters of Cornwall. They had strange names: Fat-face, Tuscan, Egyptian, and often several typefaces were used on one headstone. Churchyards such as Egloshayle and St Endellion have superb collections showing the number of typefaces which were available, many of them combining imported ideas with traditional and vernacular lettering. One of the best known sculptors was Robert Oliver of St Minver who lived from 1798 to 1872 and whose work follows the contemporary title-page, with a number of lettering styles on one slate.

From the middle of the nineteenth century there was a steady decline in the standard of design. The Industrial Revolution brought the commercialisation of quarry-cut stones of coarser outline and clumsy lettering. Towards the end of the century granite curbs filled with green marble chips began to appear, as did great granite memorials like the ones at Padstow with machine-cut letters. Foreign marbles, which neither mellow with time nor weather with nature appeared in the churchyards as the 'trade' monumental mason took over.

In our own century the characterless cemetery or churchyard extension has become the norm, but there is still good individual work being carried out. The enchanting portrayal of the Good Shepherd on William Cowling's headstone at Poundstock (1901) is a good example; there are headstones by Eric Gill at Pelynt and St Genny's. More recent is the memorial to Barbara Hepworth in St Ives, by David Kindersley. At the present time Joe Hemming of Sancreed is carrying out

Crude granite slabs 1950, Padstow

Modern headstones, Lanteglos-by-Camelford

some beautiful work which can be seen in a number of churchyards, including Lelant, Paul and Veryan. Jack Trowbridge has only recently moved to Cornwall; his work has a simple dignity, with inspired use of modern letterforms.

Both men are recommended by Memorials by Artists, an organisation which keeps a register of the best memorials artists in the country.

Their object is that people looking for a well-designed memorial can be put in touch with a suitable artist.

The Cornwall Family History Society has an ongoing programme of transcribing memorial inscriptions in all Cornish burial grounds, and have so far recorded over 250 grounds, with another 80 in progress. Volumes containing the records are available from the Society, who are always glad of help in this work.

Modern stone 1976, Lelant

Modern slate 1991, Sancreed

Broken slate with erratic spelling 1783, St Mewan

A walk round almost any of our churchyards will demonstrate the problems that face incumbents and Parochial Church Councils. Tilting, sinking headstones and crumbling chest tombs bear witness to the ravages of time and weather. The cost of repairing them all would be prohibitive and understandably many feel that the limited resources available should be spent on the fabric and maintenance of the church itself.

Collapsing tombs are a danger as well as an eyesore, and the numbers in need of repair may be in the hundreds. It worth noting that Parochial Church Councils are legally responsible for maintaining the churchyard in good repair, and may be held liable for injury caused by unsafe memorials. We were appalled to find a severely damaged chest tomb at Ruan Lanihorne where the exposed vault underneath was some twenty feet deep and could have caused serious injury to an adventurous child.

A great number of our churchyard memorials are listed, which means that they are of special interest and cannot be demolished or altered without permission. Details of listings are held by the District Council, the Record Office and the Royal Commission on Historical Monuments.

There is no automatic right to erect a memorial in a churchyard. Strictly speaking, every memorial requires a faculty, although in practice the incumbent is authorised to grant permission within certain limits. What memorials we may or may not erect in our churchyards is controlled by the diocese, who see themselves as having a responsibility to preserve their beauty and maintain some control over the introduction of inappropriate designs or materials. However they do encourage imaginative individual designs and hand-cut lettering in local slate. A copy of the Churchyard Regulations can be obtained from the Diocesan Office.

Briar and ivy damaging a superb chest tomb, Padstow

EPITAPHS

The study of epitaphs in a country churchyard provides a fascinating insight into the lives of our ancestors. They present a contemporary record not only of the facts of who died but often how they died and who mourned for them. They reflect the attitudes to death at a time of high infant mortality and killer diseases. There are good collections of epitaphs at Morwenstow, St Endellion, St Ives, St Merryn and many more.

The moral tone of earlier epitaphs is reflected in a ledger on a chest tomb at Lanteglos-by-Camelford to Mary Hodge who died in 1684 and her son who died in 1699:

> Heare lyes the mother and her hopeful son
> Their days are past, their race is run
> May you behold as well think on
> Your days doe pass and will be gone
> The grave must be your lodging place
> Be carefull them to Runn your Race
> Running so well you may obtaine
> Your dying then will be your Gaine.

An epitaph on the wall at St Eval shows how, as lettering skills developed during the eighteenth century, epitaphs became increasingly sentimental and flowery, as though the sculptors were showing off their newly-acquired skills. It has the unusual use of brackets:

> Here lyeth the body of Mary Binney the wife of Richard Binney of this Parish who died 4th July 1757 aged 37 years.
> Within the narrow confine of this Stone
> Religion, Sense and Vertue met in one
> Whose feeble Fabrick long distrest with cares
> Made her invoke her God with humble Tears
> To ease her mind, to give her soul relief
> To sooth her passions and asswage her Grief
> He graciously (becase her saw her faint)
> Dissolv'd the frame but made the soul a Saint.

In an age of high child mortality this epitaph from Landewnack is a sad memorial to three tiny children:

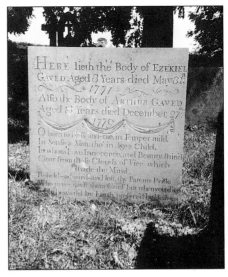

Epitaph 1771, St Mewan

> Here lie the remains of the infant twin daughters of George and Jane Burkell, who survived their birth only a few hours, also their infant son who died at the age of eleven weeks:
> Happy the babes who privileged by Fate
> To shorter labour and a lighter weight
> Received but yesterday the gift of breath,
> Ordered tomorrow to return to Death.

This slate on the east wall of St Stephen-by-Launceston has somewhat erratic spelling. It is in memory of William Bouncell and Mary his wife, 1745:

> In love wee lived to love we died
> And hear we lie each by the other's side
> Untill ye Archangell doe us forth call
> Who will awake and summons all.
> Wherefore to live and living die
> That wee to ease may all God praise and glorifie.

In the days when there was no effective relief from pain and suffering epitaphs similar to this one at St Merryn are to be found in nearly every churchyard:

The pale consumption gave the fatal blow
The stroke was certain but the effect came slow
In lingering pain Death found her sore oppressed
Gods will be done for that we know is best.

This one dated 1763 at St Teath is also common:

Affliction sore long time I bore
Physicians were in vain
Till God should please that Death should ease
And drive away our pain.

Accidental death in a nation so close to the sea is hardly surprising, and many churchyards have headstones recording shipwrecks, such as the well-known ones at Mylor and at Mawgan-in-Pydar. At Lansallos (with an identical one at Talland) is a headstone to a smuggler, John Perry, Mariner,

'who was unfortunately kill'd by a Cannon Ball by a person unknown in ye year 1779 aged 24 years, June ye 5th.
In prime of life my suddenly
Sad tidings to relate
Here view my utter destiny
And pity my sad fate.

Accidental death, Cardinham

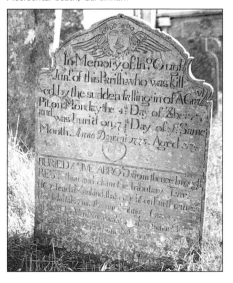

Epitaph to two small sisters 1782, Cardinham

I by a shot which rapid flew
Was instantly struck dead
Lord pardon the offender who
My precious blood did shed
Grant him to rest and forgive me
All I have done amiss
And that I may rewarded be
With everlasting bliss.

Richard Jinkin's epitaph (1793) at Linkinhorne is short and to the point:

From off an horse he then was thrown
And quickly life from him was gone.

Several headstones record foul play. In addition to the one at Egloshayle is the headstone by the south porch at St Anthony. It is in memory of an unfortunate road surveyor, Richard Roskruge, who was 'killed by a labourer with a biddaxe' in August 1797 at the age of 60. The widow's first epitaph was unacceptable to the vicar. It read:

Ah! Rueful Fate! beneath in dust I lie,
Doomed by a cruel ruffian's hand to die;
By a merciless blow he struck my brain so sure
That death ensued and lo! I am no more.

Drooping angel and pierced heart 1780, Cardinham

The one that is now on the stone was thought to be 'as breathing more of a Christian charity':

> Doomed by a neighbour's erring hand to die,
> From him my spirit breathes from Heaven a sigh!
> Oh! While repentant prayers the deed atone
> Be mine to waft them to the eternal throne!

Allegorical epitaphs are particularly appropriate to the sea, like this one at Michaelstow to William Hockin 'who exchanged Earth for Heaven' on June 7 1804, aged 24:

> Our friend is gone before
> To that celestial shore
> He hath left his mates behind
> He hath all the storms outrode
> Found the rest we toil to find
> Landed in the arms of God.

Or this one at Padstow to Samuel Gard 'of this Port' who died on 1 June 1826 aged 76:

> Now at her berth my bark is come
> And I have done with sail and tide
> Strong is my cable now I cry
> My anchor sure I safely ride
> No more my soul needs try her ground

The figure of William Bouncell 1745,
St Stephen-by-Launceston

> Safe at her mooring she is found
> And all's well.

St Ives has a rare anagram epitaph:

> Neere to this bed sixe Sises late wer laid,
> Foure hopefull sons, a grandsire and a maid,
> All striving which should end his journey first
> All for the well-spring of true Life did thirst;
> The virgin's elegy outweepes the rest,
> Such lovely grase was stampt on face and brest.

The maid died in 1642; the anagram reads:

> Alice Sise: ills cease.

There is rumoured to be an acrostic in Gunwalloe churchyard, although no-one seems able to find it. It is similar to one on a brass of 1708 to Hannibal Basset in the church at Mawgan-in-Meneage. It reads:

> Shall   weee   all   die?
> Weee   shall   die   all.
> All   die   shall   weee?
> Die   all   weee   shall.

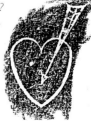

St Kew 1870

The importance of our churchyards for nature conservation is being increasingly recognised. In some parishes, with the disappearance of natural pasture the churchyard may be the only area of unimproved grassland, free of fertilisers and chemicals, an oasis of unploughed, unsprayed meadowland rich in species of wildlife and flowers. A churchyard of less than an acre may contain over a hundred different flowering plants and ferns, as well as providing a refuge for birds, insects, butterflies and moths, invertebrates and small mammals. Yet how often do we find the churchyard deep in nettles, the memorials covered in ivy? Or mown as smooth as a billiard table, with the headstones cleared to the boundary, or even worse, discarded altogether?

The flora and fauna in any one churchyard will be unique, the habitats depending on a number of variables: the aspect, the exposure to the elements, the soil type and drainage and the amount of previous management. The church building itself will support a certain amount of wildlife: from the vantage points of tower or roof owls and kestrels will prospect for their next meal. House martins, swifts and sparrows will rear their families in the nooks and crannies of the outside walls; and bats may roost and hibernate, not, as popular belief would have it, in the belfry, but in the roof. Churchyards are valuable feeding grounds for bats, as the native species of plants often found there attract the insects on which they feed. Brown Long-eared and Pipistrelle bats are the species most commonly found, while in Cornwall only one colony survives of the declining Greater Horseshoes.

Lichens and mosses will have colonised the outside walls; the six churches on the Lizard which are built of serpentine rock are particularly rich in lichens, reflecting the mineral-rich nature of the rock. At Landewednack the tower is patched with a number of colonies, and the memorials are shaggy with the salt-loving grey lichen Ramalina siliquosa, which we also found in abundance at Morwenstow. Other churchyards rich in lichens, many of them growing on trees, are St Michael's Mount, Altarnun, Towednack, Morvah and Zennor, which has the first mainland sighting of Sarcogyne Clavus, although it has since been recorded at Phillack and Gwithian. The rare Teloschistes flavicans was found on a tree in Sancreed churchyard. Lichens grow very slowly, some at only half a millimetre a year; each variety favours a particular aspect, so if stones are uprooted and moved to the boundary the lichens are likely to be destroyed.

Trees and hedges provide nesting sites for birds: rooks, tawny owls, woodpeckers and nuthatches. Trees native to Britain such as oak, ash, maple, holly, hazel or rowan, also providing winter food for birds and small mammals. Yews, most ancient and venerated of our churchyard trees, are favourite nesting sites for the greenfinch, chaffinch, mistlethrush and coal tit. Stately lime trees, often lining the paths, are very attractive to bees. Dead trees are also valuable as nesting and roosting sites for birds and bats, while rotting wood will be home to insects and fungi and a welcome source of food for woodpeckers.

Finally in some corner, discreetly hidden, will be a compost heap with old mowings warm and welcoming to insects, hedgehogs and slow-worms; a larder and a builders' merchant for birds.

However it is the grassland which is generally the cause of conflict. Those who would like to see it mown as smooth as a bowling green imagine that conservation is synonymous with neglect and that long grass, nettles and brambles will be allowed to take over. In fact all conservation is of course a compromise which may well reduce the amount of work involved, at the same time allowing different areas to provide for a varied range of wildlife and flowers.

The most efficient way to embark on a new plan of management is to make a survey; in that way the wildlife already taking advantage of the habitats will not be disturbed and the needs of people using the churchyard will be respected. The aim should be to provide a balance, with areas of grass of different lengths providing different habitats. At the approach to the church and in areas where access is needed, such as where graves are still being tended or where cremation plaques are placed, the grass should be kept short. The cuttings should be raked off so that new growth is not smothered. In areas of longer grass where spring flowers grow, the grass should not be cut until June, by which time the plants will have flowered and set seed and the new generations of butterflies will have flown. It can then be cut again in October to leave it ready for the following spring.

Summer flowering meadow should be cut in the spring between April and June, then left through the summer and cut again in late autumn. The mowings should be raked off after every cutting, or the decaying grass will encourage the growth of rank grass at the expense of flowers.

Obviously most parts of the churchyard will have flowers that span the whole season and it will be necessary to identify which ones are important and plan accordingly. Many of the traditional churchyard and meadow flowers such as cowslips and harebells can be raised from seed. Small areas should be left totally uncut, perhaps along the boundary, to provide cover for small mammals, amphibians, lizards, and slow worms.

A number of Cornish parishes have now recorded the flowering plants, ferns, trees and shrubs in their churchyards: Devoran and Kenwyn have over 50 species, Lanteglos-by-Fowey and St Breock over 70. At Lanteglos-by-Camelford, where we found wild strawberries growing on a chest tomb, and at Launcells there were notices in the churchyards indicating that certain areas were set aside for conservation. At Lanteglos-by-Fowey the Parochial Church Council has set up a Churchyard Guild - representatives of the parish who sit with the PCC and advise them on matters of archaeology, history and conservation.

At one time neglected and overgrown rural churchyards would rapidly have been recolonised from the surrounding farmland, but the advent of mechanised farming with its chemicals and fertilizers, together with the decimation of hedgerows, means that accidental colonisation can no longer be left to chance.

The Church and Conservation Project, based at Stoneleigh, promotes sympathetic churchyard management for wildlife. Their Living Churchyard pack provides information on all aspects of churchyard management, including training days within the dioceses.

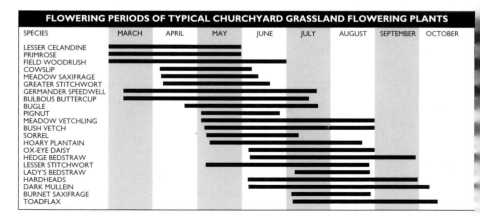

FLOWERING PERIODS OF TYPICAL CHURCHYARD GRASSLAND FLOWERING PLANTS

SPECIES	MARCH	APRIL	MAY	JUNE	JULY	AUGUST	SEPTEMBER	OCTOBER
LESSER CELANDINE								
PRIMROSE								
FIELD WOODRUSH								
COWSLIP								
MEADOW SAXIFRAGE								
GREATER STITCHWORT								
GERMANDER SPEEDWELL								
BULBOUS BUTTERCUP								
BUGLE								
PIGNUT								
MEADOW VETCHLING								
BUSH VETCH								
SORREL								
HOARY PLANTAIN								
OX-EYE DAISY								
HEDGE BEDSTRAW								
LESSER STITCHWORT								
LADY'S BEDSTRAW								
HARDHEADS								
DARK MULLEIN								
BURNET SAXIFRAGE								
TOADFLAX								

GAZETEER

ALTARNUN

The church stands in an attractive corner of the village with the stream running under the old bridge and a mounting block planted with flowers by the church wall. Handsome wrought iron gates between granite pillars lead into the churchyard, with a Celtic wheelhead cross by the path.

South of the chancel is a slate carved with a nail by Nevill Northey Burnard, sculptor, a rare mediaeval signature with his age, 14. It has the figure of an eagle flying in the rays of the sun, and a sprig of rosemary. It is a memorial to his grandparents who died in 1745 and is beautifully lettered in serifs, italics and script.

A row of stones by the east wall has been nicely re-set in the grass. The one to Thomas Nicholls dated 1766 is also by Nevill Northey Burnard who made several slate headstones when he was young. At the top is a skeleton with arrow and shovel, in the middle a trumpeting bosomed angel and on the right another skeleton with scythe and hourglass. It reads:

> Mortals repent while in the bloom of day
> Fly to a pardoning God without delay
> Go wash with me in Jesus' cleansing blood
> This, this alone can make you meet for God.
> My days are past, my time is at an end
> I go to meet my Everlasting Friend.
> His Grace prepar'd me for His Courts above
> There I shall praise Him to His dying Love.

On the south wall of the church is a slate with two angels and a heart in memory of James Matthew of this Parish. He 'died 27th January in the year of our Lord 1754 aged 21 and likewise his daughter Grace.' The epitaph is written in a flowing script:

> In bloom of years we lost our vital breath
> And soon were cut down by obdurate Death
> To dust must all both pomp and riches come
> And as we now lie mouldering in the Tomb
> Tho vapour-like our lives soon vanish'd be
> We fly to Christ for none can save but He
> His Arms are willing to receive a bove
> All weary souls that Glory in His Love.

BLISLAND

Blisland is a place of great antiquity, rich in wayside crosses. Nearby is the stone circle called Nine Trippet Stones, also a set of seven stone crosses from early Christianity, one of which is

Gateway and tower, Altarnun

now in the churchyard. The church is the only one in England to be dedicated to St Proteus and St Hyacinth, third century martyrs.

Above the door the sundial has an angel and was cut by Christopher Lean in 1780. His own headstone is in the churchyard along with other members of his family. He died in 1826 at the age of 62 and his epitaph reads:

Farewell vain world, I know enough of thee,
And now am careless of what thou say'st of me.
Thy Smiles I caught not nor thy Frowns I fear,
My Cares are past, my head lies quiet here
What Faults you know in me take care to shun,
And look at home, enough there's to be done.

(SIGNED P SIBLY)

A slate on the west wall of the church has winged angels in the spandrels; it is in memory of John Rogers, yeoman, who died in 1781. In the corner by the porch is another which reads:

Heare lieth the body of John Drakes who died ye
11th day of May 1780 aged 36 years.

The churchyard is full of nineteenth century patternbook headstones, excellent examples of the skills of the craftsmen of the period. One commemorating another member of the Rogers family, William F Rogers, is dated 1876 and has a weeping angel in relief.

The lives of much-loved parents, Peter Kingdon who died in 1848 aged 60 and his wife Susanna

Mourning angel, Blisland

Waving figure 1848, St Breock

are fondly remembered:

Fond and loved and full of of days
We laid them in the silent earth
And here this humble stone we raise
A tribute to our parents worth.

ST BREOCK

The church of St Breock has an enormous sloping churchyard full of tall trees, with beech nuts crunching underfoot. At the north entrance is a lych gate; the east entrance, where a stream runs through the churchyard, has a pretty wrought iron arch and lamp. The ground is carpeted with ivy and celandines, the birdsong deafening.

The churchyard has a good collection of eighteenth century headstones; the one to Richard Lobb, dated 1761, has a skeleton and pierced hearts in the spandrels; carved round the curve is the legend: 'Death with his Dart hath pierced his heart'. Among the nineteenth century slates is a ledger to Jane, wife of Thomas Key, 1854, by Robert Oliver of St Minver, an excellent example of the influence of the contemporary engraved title page. Nearby is a headstone to Richard Blake, 1848, with a figure in a loose dress unmistakeably waving farewell, carved in relief. Another stone recalls a much-loved daughter by name:

Headstone with mixed lettering 1793, St Buryan

*Here lieth the body of Roger Harris of this Parish
who departed this life the 14th day of March
1792 in the 40th year of his Age.
Dear wife I now from you must go
And my dear Bab's must leave also.
Though short my Time on Earth to stay
Twas God's command I must a way.
So mourn no more I pray for me
A better place I hope to see,
Where you and I shall there remain
And my dear Babs ne'er part again.*

On the north side of the church is a stone which
reminds us of the hazards of Cornwall's
traditional industries. It is to Nicholas Webber
who was injured at Great Wheal Busy Mine
and died at Chacewater on 16th January
1859 aged 45 years.

ST BURYAN

St Buryan is an ancient circular churchyard;
with its high position it was certainly
an important religious site in Norman
times and probably earlier. It is
possible that the circular
boundary represents the
outline of an Iron
Age earthwork.

The Domesday Book records a religious
community at St Buryan. In modern times its 92
ft tower in flowing Perpendicular lines is a
notable landmark.

In 1985 a small archaeological excavation was
carried out when part of the churchyard wall was
demolished and the road widened. The remains
of two or three earlier walls were found as well
as a single shard of Iron Age or Romano-British
pottery, a prehistoric flint scraper and a number
of post-mediaeval artefacts.

The modern churchyard has a good collection of
eighteenth and nineteenth century stones. There
are two crosses, one by the south door from the
tenth century standing on more recent steps,
another outside the south gate carved with the
figure of Christ, his feet turned outwards. There
is also a mounting block with six steps on each
side.

The porch has a slate sundial dated 1747.
Nearby on the outside church wall is some
excellent eighteenth century work on slate. One
of them is a gentle message from his wife in
memory of Thomas Williams 'who died May
30th 1795 in the 80th year of his age':

*Sleep here awhile
Thou Dearest Part of me;
In little Time
I'll come and sleep with thee.*

By the south path is an allegorical epitaph to
Captain William Simpson who was drowned
near St Just in 1867:

*Our life is but a winter's day
Some only breakfast and away.
Others to dinner stay and are full fed,
The oldest only sups and goes to bed,
Large is his debt who lingers out the day
Who goes the soonest has the least to
pay.*

St Buryan

Celtic wheelhead cross, Cardinham

CARDINHAM

Two crosses stand in the churchyard of St Meubred, both formerly built into the east wall of the chancel. The Celtic wheel cross which dates from the ninth or tenth century is described by Langdon as 'one of the best preserved of its kind in the county.' It is eight and a half feet high with knotwork on the front face and interlace on the back. The second is a wheelhead cross with projections and was originally a grave marker. There is a slate sundial dated 1739 and stocks inside the porch.

A stone with a shaped top and an angel is in memory of Ino Ough Jn who was 'killed by the sudden falling in of a Grave Pit' in 1775 at the age of 37. The epitaph has the usual erratic spacing, the words on the right margin being crammed in, and is partly indecipherable:

Buried Alive Abro'd and from thence brought here.
Rest thou and claim the tributary Tear,
Here teach Mankind that nought on Earth can save
Poor Mortals from the unrelenting Grave.
All, all is Vain,nor wealth nor health nor strength
To human Life can add one Moment's length.
Hence go to God for thy Saviour's sake.

A broad stone with an enigmatic angel and a pierced heart commemorates the death of Roger

Bate who died on 7th November 1780 aged 21.

I was a flourishing young plant
All in my youthful prime;
I now I'em to Death and Dust
Twas God's appointed time.
My parents dear and sisters near
Of you I take farewell,
And rest in hope to meet again
In Heav'n for to dwell.

Also John and Rebecca Bate aged eight and two years respectively.

ST CLEMENT

The church stands in a picturesque corner of the village with thatched cottages and spilling flowers. The lych gate has an overhanging room with eighteenth-century slates on the walls where they are well protected from the elements. They represent beautiful examples of the lettering of the period, complete with endearing mistakes in spelling and spacing:

In memory of Mary the wife of John Devonshire who died September 23rd 1777 aged 23:

Adieu blessd partner of my life
A tender faithfull Loving Wife
When follow hope to meet thee where
No pain nor parting interfere.

And another looking as fresh as the day it was carved:

In memory of William Callaway who departed this life July 18th 1784 aged 45 years:

Headstone with epitaph 1784, St Clement

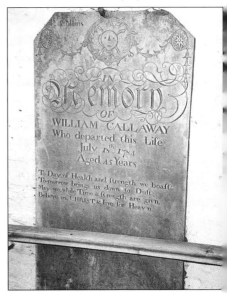

To Day of health and strength we boast
Tomorrow brings us down to Dust
May we while time and strength are giv'n
Believe in Christ and live for Heaven.

A beautiful slate with a border carved in relief is a memorial to Thomas Petherick James who died on 14th February 1779 aged 3 years, and a daughter Mary James who died on 1st March 1779 aged 5 years:

What solemn sorrow must we now Devise
To join those tears which trickle from our eyes
Alas, no more on Earth we'll here their voice
Which made the heavenly Choire to Rejoice
Oh, could we raise them from their silent sleep
With tears of blood our watry eyes shoud weep.
But hold, forbear our sorrows to exclaim
On what conducts them to Eternal Fame.

Just inside the churchyard two large slates lean against the wall, sadly broken; the date is 1722:

Not dead but sleeping on our Mother's brest
Wrapt in her Bosom, here we take our rest
Till trumpets sound ye Angels Cry appear
Then rise shall we and stay no longer here.

Also a stone to John Taylor dated 1832 who seems happy to have departed this life:

Farewell to all beneath the sun
I bid the world adieu
I never found no solid mirth

Pious inscription 1846, Egloshayle

Nor happiness in you.

The church has gargoyles on the tower and a tall inscribed stone of AD 500-550 by the door with the inscription on the shaft: IGNIOC VITALI FILI TORRICI, as well as an Ogham inscription. It was re-cut as a cross in the eighth century.

EGLOSHAYLE

A pleasant, level churchyard with a lych gate on the north side. It contains an exceptional collection of eighteenth century slates with good examples of lettering, many of them signed by Robert Oliver. In particular there are several slates with shadowed lettering.

There is a sad epitaph to John Broad who died 25th December 1831 aged 2. What a terrible Christmas present for his family.

Sweet blossom doom'd in early life to fade
And lie neglected in the gloomy shade
Yet thou shalt spring again, in beauty rise
To grace the flowery scenes of Paradise.

An odd shaped headstone records a brutal crime:

To Nevell Norway, merchant of Wadebridge aged 39 who was murdered on the 8th February 1840.
He left behind him a widow and six children unprovided for. A subscription of £3,500 was made for their use, a noble testimony of the generous feeling of the public and the high estimation in which his amiable and spotless character was held.

Attached to the east wall of the church are five slate stone in a solid block, all commemorating the Lakeman family who died in the mid-1800's. Next to them is a very nice stone to Grace Will who died in 1817. It is signed by J Arthur, engraver:

Forgive blest shade thy tributary tear
That mourns thy exit from a world like this.
Forgive the wish that would have kept thee here
And stay'd thy progress to the seats of bliss.
No more confin'd to growling scenes of night,
No more a tenant penn'd in mortal clay,
Now shall we rather Hail thy glorious flight
And trace thy Journey to the realms of day.

The west door of the tower is carved with snakes in the roll-moulding of the jambs, a curious Celtic survival. An undated slate with attractive lettering on the south wall of the church reads:

Whoever is seen loitering in the churchyard or behaving indecently during Divine Service will be prosecuted according to Law.

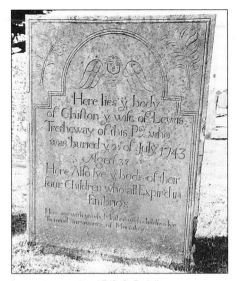

Interesting wording 1743, St Endellion

ST ENDELLION

Another pleasant, level churchyard with an outstanding collection of stones illustrating the development of the art of letter-cutting. Among the oldest and most decorative is a ledger by the chancel wall to Catherine and Elizabeth Billing, with angels in the spandrels, dated 1717. The lettering was done without much forward planning, and some of the words have had to be squeezed in:

> Death with his dart did pierce our hearts
> When we were in our prime,
> Our parents dear your grief forbear
> Twas God's appointed time.
> That time when we were to remove
> To Jesus Christ and saints above'
> With them to live and praises sing
> To all wise Eternal King.

Next to it is another to the four children of William and Margarita Rouse who all died in the 1860's. Unusually, the spandrels are carved in relief. The gruesome epitaph reads:

> In pain and sickness long we laid
> Our flesh consum'd, our lungs decay'd;
> We like flowers once did bloom
> Now lie mould'ring in the tomb.

A very nice stone with eighteenth century lettering records the death of Chilton, ye wife of Lewis Trethaway at the age of 37 in 1743. It says:

> Here also lye ye bodis of their four Children who
> all Expir'd in Embrio's.
> Here age with youth, Mother with children lye
> To mind Survivours of Mortality.

Among a number of good mid-nineteenth century stones is one to Hannah Fishley with shadowed lettering signed by Adams; a stone to William Leay who was '(casually) drowned' in 1869 and several title-page stones including one to William Kellow of Port Isacc who died in 1855. On the same stone his son Robert, Master Mariner, was lost at sea in 1856 aged 32 years.

ST ENODOC

This little churchyard has a very special feel; it is quite on its own overlooking Daymer Bay. For years the church with its crooked spire was almost entirely overwhelmed by sand, and a service was held only once a year, with the clergymen let into the church through a skylight. There used to be a Roman oratory at the foot of Brea Hill and the remains of a mediaeval village have been found between the church and the sea, from which came the domestic mortars which line the church path. It also contains the graves of Sir John Betjeman, much loved Poet Laureate and Cornishman, who rests beneath a decorated modern slate, and his mother.

The entrance has a lych gate and coffin slab, and a little building that was once a mortuary. Outside the south porch is an ancient chest tomb; the ledger that was on it is now in the porch, a charming memorial to John Mably and daughter Alice who died in 1687 within six days of each other. It has portraits of them both, he in knickerbockers and she in a dress with a laced

Ancient cross, Feock

Lych gate with upper room, Feock

bodice and full skirt. It is said to be the latest known incised slab with effigies. The inscription reads:

Remember man within thy youthfull days
To serve the Lord eare death thy body seize
Then Live to dye to came soe high a price
That thy poor soule may Live in Paradise
Here is the Love of my Wife Shone that where
wee ly by this it may be known
my wife and I did in Love So well agree
Yet must I part For God
Would have it so to be.

There are several headstones to the Mably family, who were evidently local people of some importance. One has beautiful even script closely written:

In memory of John Mably of Trebetherick yeoman
who died on ye 9th day of March 1800 at 61
and his wife Joan and their daughter Joanna who
was buried in 1789 aged 18 years.
Death and the grave doth summons all away
From hence and none can answer him with nay
Death calls both rich and poor unto ye ground
Both kings and queens all from the Princely Crowns
Death calls us hence unto Gods Judgment Aright
From this dark reigon to that glorious light
Where Christ and angels there they sing
Sweet Hallelujas to ye King of kings.

ST ERTH

A restful churchyard with flowers and shrubs shaded by tall trees. On the corners of the tower grotesque dogs lean out as though reading the headstones.

The vault of the Hawkins family is built into the bank at the east end of the church. It is surmounted by a sarcophagus with moulded feet, an urn at one end and a chest tomb at the other. Against the wall of the gully at the east end of the church are some eighteenth century slates with highly skilled lettering, even if the spacing is somewhat erratic. One of them has an heraldic crest cut in relief; it is in memory of William Davies of Bosworgy in this Parish who died in 1690 aged 54. The long epitaph begins:

Must Death divide us now and close thine eyes
How shall I live when thou art gone to hear our
children's cries
Look on but spare your tears, forbear to weep
My Death's no Death in Christ, a blessed sleep

A big slate against the same wall is carved with an urn and two roundels. The epitaph has a metaphorical message:

Near this stone is intr'd the remains of john
Rowe of Trevin, Gent, who departed this life june
24th aged 79 and Luce his wife who departed
this life December 1714 aged 62.
O Lord what a feeble worm is man
That like a flower doth fade
He cometh up and is cut down
Beneath night's sable shade
To Thee dear Lord our precious souls
We joyfully resigne
Blessed Jesus take us for thine own
For we are ever Thine.

Cast iron memorials, St Erth

Several of the stones are signed by John Trevaskis, Sculptor of St Erth.

By the gate is a small kerbed area and a slate which reads:

> Within this enclosure lie interred the bodies of six persons who in the year 1832 died of the awful visitation of cholera.

Another nearby records the death of Amos Dabb who 'for fifty years was schoolmaster in this parish.' Other occupations are Roger Wearn, watch and clockmaker, who died in 1820 and has a rather worn slate on the church wall; also Jochebe Hockin, who was in the service of one family from 1750 until she died in 1814 aged 86. Under the trees is a little cluster of cast iron memorials, all similar, and nearly all of them in memory of small children.

FORRABURY

From the hill above Boscastle, the church at Forrabury and its surrounding churchyard is a rectangle alone on the cliff. An ancient cross which stands outside the churchyard is not in its original position. By the gate is a stone to William Keals 'who for 54 years officiated as Clark(sic) to the Parish of Minster and Forrabury.' He was buried May 27 1838 aged 88 years.

In the gully under the east wall of the church is a seventeenth century stone, now unfortunately broken, which tells of a son who followed his mother to the grave in 1647. The sad little rhyme reads:

> A true and welcome guest; to whom I gave
> My life, my whole, should I deny my grave?

Next to the broken stone is one written in Latin with an odd-looking angel, a pierced heart and an hour glass. By the path is a stone which reads:

> Here lyeth ye body of Agnes ye wife of John Gard who was buried 31st August 1786.
> My dearest Husband lo I come
> To meet thee in eternal home,
> To dwell above in Christ's embrace
> And to behold him face to face.
> Tis only from the Lord above
> A gracious act of foreign love.

The fish weathervane on the tower reminds us that this is a maritime community. So does the memorial to Thomas Henry Danger 'who perished by the upsetting of a boat near Boscastle on April 16th 1858 aged 17 years. While deploring his untimely death his relatives and friends are comforted by the remembrance of his youth and obedience.

> Our life is like the grass
> Our youth is like the flower
> They rise, they bloom and then Alas!
> They perish in an hour.

Angel and epitaph 1786, Forrabury

ST JUST-IN-ROSELAND

This is a steep bowl of a churchyard, full of shrubs and flowers, pleasantly overgrown, with the church at the bottom, its toes almost in the water. The twin lych gates have seats and bargeboards, the bottom one almost on the beach with an enormous stone cattle grid leading to the Holy Well and spring. In the top lych gate, which dates from 1632 is an appropriate message:

> Here rest the silent dead and here too I,
> When yonder dial shall strike the hour must lie.
> Look round! Like orderly array
> See, where the buried Host await the Judgement Day.
> Stranger in peace pursue thine onward road
> But ne'er forget thy last and long abode.

As usual the oldest stones are on the south side of the church:

> Here lyes the bodyes of the daughters of Mr John Rice and Thomazin his wife, Agnes Rice departed this life the 16th day of February 1752 aged 1 year, Ann Rice departed this life the 8th day of April 1751 aged 2 years.

And next to it:

> Margerey Terrill the wife of Johnson Terrill who departed this life the 19th day of February 1757 aged 83 years. Here also lyeth the body of the above Johnson Terrill. Hee departed this life the 10th day of January 1758 aged 82 years. Their children died during an epidemic of diphtheria.

Like to ripe fruit when nothing can them save
When from mortal fate they drop't into their
Grave.

A plaque on the east wall of the church commemorates William Fittock, mayor of St Mawes, who 'had the stature of an Oak tree and was of great physical strength' and his daughter Mary who died at the age of seven. Higher in the churchyard are some neat modern slates, effective and inoffensive. One remembers the life of Jonathon Hugh Price, poet, 1931-85; another to Dora M Clifford-Wing of St Mawes 1879-1971 says simply:

God loves us. He made us. He keeps us.

ST KEVERNE

St Keverne stands by the village square, with magnificent views over Falmouth Bay and beyond. This churchyard is a memorial, literally, to hundreds of men amd women shipwrecked on this treacherous coast; the two little creatures carved in the west doorway of the tower seem to reflect something of the savagery of the elements. The Carronade by the lych gate was recovered from the wreck of the troop carrier *Primrose* which together with the *Dispatch* was wrecked during the Napoleonic Wars in 1809.

Another stone marks the burial site of 193 men, women and children who died when the emigrant ship *John* went down on the Manacles on May 3rd 1855 en route for Canada.

Nearby is the memorial to 'Charles Cecil Brown, London, SW England' who was lost in the wreck of the SS *Mohegan* on October 14th 1898. He was a devoted and only son to his widowed mother and 'never said an unkind word to her in his life.' His stone stands near the cross that commemorates the 100 men who drowned in 20 minutes when the ship foundered.

A slate to John Bastian who died on May 13th 1835 aged 55 years describes his unexpected death:

It was so suddenly I fell
My neighbours started at my Knell
Amazed that I should be no more
The man obeyed seen the day before
But what security is breath
Against the uplifted hand of Death
Not one is safe, not one secure
Not one can call his moment sure
Be wise and let that holy path be daily used
In which without surprise a man may meet his
God.

Lych gate and church, St Just-in-Roseland

Primrose memorial 1809, St Keverne

No surname, no date, Kilkhampton

A nicely lettered stone commemorates James Pearce who was unfortunately killed by a rock falling on him 3rd November 1801 aged 42 years; another, now lying flat, to John Williams, who died in 1790 aged 33 years has a distinctly fateful tone:

> How lov'd, how valued once
> Avail's thee not
> By whom related or by whom begot
> A heap of dust alone remains of thee.

KILKHAMPTON

A large, level churchyard, 800 feet above the sea. The handsome lych gate still has its coffin slab and the paths are lined with trees. There are good eighteenth century stones in front of the church and some with decorated tops along the south wall. One of them has an angel and reads:

> In memory of William Trick of Scadghill whose body was interred ye 19th day of May 1731 in ye 52nd year of his age, And likewise of Jane ye wife of ye above.

One little boy was obviously not destined for a long life. He was William the son of Thomas and Susanne Cleave who died in 1825 at the age of three.

> My life was short, my days were few
> A cripple while I was with you;
> Till Christ did call to soar above
> To dwell in everlasting love.

The sexton directed us to the grave of Henry Everitt Mattison, 1875–1930, an American who was travelling in London and asked as he died to be buried here. He lies looking towards America with no land between his grave and his distant homeland. His stone reads simply:

> He brought happiness to his family and friends.

A stone in well-cut script has no visible date or dedication, yet it bears a heartfelt epitaph to two children:

> In heaven where Infants Hail
> Their mighty King
> There little William and Joanna sing
> Their Virgin Souls
> Straight entered Paradise
> Dreading no let
> Because they knew no vice.
> Too good for Earth
> They soon shook off their day
> And to Immortal Glory winged their way.

In a corner of the churchyard are the graves of three men whose bodies were washed ashore from a ship torpedoed in the War.

There are a number of occupations mentioned on the stones in the churchyard, including Lawrence Harward, Malster and Draper, 1817; Richard Grigg, Captain in the Royal Navy, 1836; and Orlando Jolliffe, Butcher, 1804.

LANIVET

Lanivet is described by Pevsner as 'one of the most rewarding places in Cornwall for information, or at least impressions, of the Dark Age from the 6th to the 10th century.' As the geographical centre of Cornwall, Christian missionary routes both north-to-south and east-to-west would have passed through Lanivet. The circular churchyard indicates an ancient site and would account for the unusual number of crosses in the vicinity.

By the south wall of the church is a rare tenth century hogback tombstone with a key-patterned gable and bear-like beasts at each end. To the west of the church is one of the finest decorated four-holed crosses; in the centre of the churchyard stands a fine wheelhead cross with primitive incised decoration which includes a man with a tail.

Carved cross, Lanivet

The headstones have all been moved to the boundary. One of them, carved with two angels and beautiful lettering, is in memory of Elizabeth and Joan Thomas, aged two and ten respectively, who died February 3rd and March 10th, 1782.

The third of February, both were alive together;
The 12th of March they lay here by each other;
Hard was ye Fate! Parents and them to fever;
But still we rest in hope they're blest forever.

Underneath like a child's drawing is a skeleton holding an hourglass and arrow. Next to it is a similar one with a fierce angel, presumably the work of the same man:

Here lieth ye body of Nathaniel (ye son of Tho. and Philippa Lane) ye Par. of St Mabyn, who was bury'd ye 29 March 1765 in the 52nd Year of his age.
With patience to the last he did Submit
And murmur'd not at what ye Lord thought fit;
He with a Christian Courage did resign
His Soul to God at his appointed Time.

LELANT

Lelant was a seaport in the Middle Ages, until outdone by St Ives, and the position of the churchyard over the Hayle estuary, dotted with boats, is most attractive.

Covering a niche over the porch is an eighteenth century Delabole slate sundial. The gnomon has an odd-looking skeleton holding an hourglass.

A memorial slab mounted on the church wall is made of a fine, hard slate which is still as sharp as the day it was cut; the border has springing foliage and flowers with a tapering scalloped edge. The word 'Memory' is highly decorated in flowing lines. The inscription is to Captain Richard Curgenven of the Royal Navy, who died on August 30th 1784 aged 47. A space has been left beneath as though expecting another inscription and it is signed by Richard Osman of Truro.

Near it is a slate on the wall to Alice Sampson who died in 1705 aged 63. It has a small grammatical error:

As you are now so once was me
As I am now so you must be
Therefore prepare to follow me.

A stone near the porch records the lives of three small children:

Mary the daughter of William and Mary Mayn who died 18th March 1803 aged 9 months, also Sarah Mayn who departed this life 18th March 1807 aged 10 weeks also Samuel Mayn who departed this life 22 May 1808 aged 4 yrs.
Beneath this little heap of earth
These harmless infants lie

18th century skeleton sundial, Lelant

Snatch'd from this world by early death
To live above the skies.
What Myriads of the aged Tribe
When souls to flesh unite
May wish they had when infants
Or never seen the light.

In the south east corner by the porch is the severely plain railed sarcophagus to William Praed who died in 1833 at the age of 84.

Under the trees in the newer section of the churchyard is a beautiful modern stone to Olive Bivar. It has a slate insert in granite carved with a Celtic cross in a plaited circle and is by Joe Hemmings.

ST LEVAN

The church of St Levan is away from the village down a winding lane with panoramic views of the sea below. The little church leans into the hillside, with a stone stile on to the footpath. Beside it is a cross with a diminutive shaft and a dominant head. The other entrance has a Cornish cattle grid and a coffin slab in the remains of a lych gate.

By the path to the porch is a fine cross standing 6 feet 11 inches high, in its original position, and said by Langdon to be one of the most elegantly proportioned in Cornwall. Nearby is the rock known as St Levan's Stone; legend has it that St Levan, thought to have been a sixth- or seventh century Celt, lived on a diet of one fresh fish a day. He used to rest on the rock when tired from fishing. One day as an old man he took his rod and struck the stone, which broke in two. He

prayed over the stone and made the prophecy:
When with panniers astride,
A Pack Horse can ride
Through St Levan's Stone,
The world will be done.

An attractive stone dated 1810 is carved with shells, flowers and, unusually, a crown. Another one is in memory of David and Elizabeth Rawlings and 'another boy unfortunately drowned:'
The happy souls have took their flight
To the blest regions of delight
Their Saviour to Adore.
Parents prepare while you are here
To meet your babes in Glory there
Where parting is no more.

MADRON

Madron has a mediaeval wheelhead cross and a lych gate which is a Boer War memorial. Stone faces look down from the outside of the chancel wall; beneath them is a beautifully decorated slate to William Thomas who died in 1781. Nearby is an old slate ledger to Thomas Hosking who died 1726, his daughter who died the same year as a baby, and his son who died in 1742. It is damaged but the epitaph begins:
Our tears attend you to the shades below
Badge of our love and monuments of woe
Tears at your tomb, deep flowing tears are paid
It's fruitless all since in the dust you're laid.

Beautiful carving 1810, St Levan

Blindfold maiden with lyre, Madron 1929

By the porch is a chest tomb in memory of Alexander Daniel, a Belgian whose stone reads:

Belgium me birth, Britain me breeding gave,
Cornwall a wife, ten children and a grave.

The school room which forms part of the churchyard boundary was established by him. To the north-east of the churchyard is an enormous memorial to John Scobell Armstrong who died in 1929. On top of it, sitting on a huge granite sphere, is the copper figure of a blindfold maiden plucking at a lyre with a broken strings.

A broken string and through the drift
Of aeons sad with human cries
She waits the Hand of God to lift
The bandage from her eyes.

This almost dwarfs the plain square Greek-style mausoleum to the Price family, built in 1820. A slate pegged to the north wall is in memory of Thomas Tresythe who died in 1806, carved with angels and trumpets, and another south of the porch is carved in relief with a bosomed figure.

MAWGAN-IN-MENEAGE

The church of St Mawgan stands in a superb position, with winged corbels on the fifteenth century tower, topped by pinnacles each with four tiny finials. The west door to the tower has leaf-scroll decoration and the keystone of the window above is carved with a small figure of the village saint. Tufts of thrift growing out of the string-course on the tower made a touch of colour against the granite.

A little building forming part of the boundary was once used as a vestry. At the south entrance to the churchyard is a pillar sundial dated 1695.

An epitaph records the death of John Trounson 'who was killed by the discharge of his gun in the act of loading' on the 14th March 1845 aged 38 years:

The stroke swifter than any arrows flight
Beyond forebodings wing'd him midway cast
Upon the swelling floods to struggle for the brighter shore
Whither we hope he reach'd
In peace and safety reader, death is sure,
And what if such a sudden death be thine?

And another to Elizabeth Curnow who died on June 10th 1860 aged 50.

A loving wife now lieth here
A tender mother, kind, sincere,
In love she lived till Death did call,
Resign'd her breath and died in Peace with all.

By the path is the splendid sarcophagus to James Alexander, Gent. The inscription reads:

This monument was erected at the expense of Mrs Anne Ingersoll, the Widow of Lieut Joseph Lander as a memorial of esteem and respect for her relative James Lander, Gent, whose property

Sarcophagus, Mawgan-in-Meneage

her family succeeded in retaining after an expensive lawsuit promoted by his distant relatives, but which by a sentence of a Judge of the Court proved to be groundless and fallacious. An elderly gentleman in his Sunday best was going to church for the morning service. He said, 'They always built the church in the most beautiful part of the parish, and they never slipped up here, did they?' He told me that in another three years he would have been a bellringer in that same church for 60 years.

MAWGAN-IN-PYDAR

The lychgate at the church of St Mawgan has a diminutive coffin stone which is a replacement. The original one was found to be a fifteenth century altar and was placed in the sanctuary. Nearby is a Holy Well, thought to be where St Mawgan first preached in the valley.

The treasure of this churchyard is the mediaeval lantern cross c.1420 with canopied niches showing the Annunciation on the west side and the Crucifixion on the east. Another cross in the rose garden is a roadside cross brought from Mawgan Cross in 1942. The wheel cross to the right of the path was found in a pigsty in 1905.

In the shape of the stern of a boat is an unusual memorial to ten men who drifted ashore on 15th December 1846 and were found frozen to death in the morning. One of them, Jemmy, has no surname. They were the first men buried under a new law which decreed that shipwrecked bodies should be buried at public expense, with rewards for those who found them. The present memorial is a beautifully carved replica of the original.

A headstone with angels in the spandrels is a memorial to Jane May, who died on 2nd of July 1799 aged 48. The epitaph reflects the grief of her loved ones:

Farewell our sister dear with grief of heart
Since God has so decreed thet we must part;
Tear's sigh's or cry's by us tis all in vain
Our loudest cries can't call her back again;
While here on Earth our care shall be to thrive,
To live like her a pious godly life,
That when we die our Souls to Heav'n may fly
To rest with Christ to all Eternity.

Another stone reminds us of the terrible toll of infant mortality:

Here rest the bodies of eight sons and daughters of James and Elizabeth Gill.

They died between 1829 and 1835; there are two Davids and two Marias; it was not uncommon to give the names of dead children to subsequent ones, a practice we would find strange.

In the corner of the churchyard is an ancient thorn tree, taken as a cutting from the Holy Thorn of Glastonbury.

Boat memorial 1846, Mawgan-in-Pydar

Home-made memorial 1837, St Mewan

ST MEWAN

St Mewan is a big churchyard with lots of yew trees and a good collection of eighteenth century slates and chest tombs. Opposite the porch is a slate with pedantic wording to Samuel Richards who died in 1811 at the age of 26:

> The language of his mind was, Oh that my words were written, Oh that they were printed in a book! That they were graven with an iron pan and laid in a rock for ever! For I know that my redeemer liveth and that he shall stand at the latter day upon the Earth. And though after my death worms destroy this body, yet in my flesh shall I see God whom I shall see for myself and mine eyes shall behold and not another though my veins be consumed within me.

This slate records the grief of parents over the loss of two sons:

> Here lies the body of Ezekiel Gavid aged three years who died May 31st 1771. Also the body of Arthur Gavid aged 13 years died December 27th 1779.
> O born to bless and die in temper mild
> In sense a man, though in age a child
> In whom love, innocence and beauty shin'd
> Clear from those clouds of vice which shade the mind
> Beheld, admitted and lost thy parents' pride
> Who never gav'st grief but when you died
> Justly bewail'd by Earth, prefer'd by Heaven
> Wherein a better, happier state is giv'n.

A slate records the death of William Treniere of St Austell 'who unfortunately fell over a cliff and was killed on the 15th day of January 1822 aged 20 years.'

In 1837 William Hill produced a home-made stone with a strange urn in memory of Fanny his wife who died at the age of 43, leaving a husband and seven children to lament their loss. The epitaph is crudely written in handwriting:

> Beneath this stone my partner sleep
> With tears of grief I fixt it
> Her former kindness make me weep
> When I behold our children dear.
> She was took from me in her prime
> And I am left behind to pine.

ST MINVER

A church stood on this site in Saxon times, and crude slate coffins have been found in the churchyard. The present church has one of the most attractive approaches: a path lined with old cottages, with through the lych gate a glimpse of the leaning spire of St Menefreda's and the eighteenth sundial over the porch. Many of the nineteenth century stones are the work of Robert Oliver, an skilled engraver who was born in this parish and lived and worked in North Cornwall until his death in 1872.

A small headstone on the west side of the churchyard commemorates Humphry Craddock who died August 5th 1787 aged four. Sadly the lettering is worn and difficult to read.

Nearby is a stone which has an angel, her hair blowing in the wind, and a skull with teeth. It is beautifully lettered in a flowing script in memory of Eleanor Legoe who died on December 7th 1792:

> Here lyeth the Husband and the Wife a Sister and a Brother
> Who friendly neighbours where to all a pattern for all other
> No oaths nor lies nor passions fire by them were spread abroad
> But when afflicting trials came resign'd their Wills to God,
> They truly serv'd the Lord above, were Just to all mankind,
> Before grim Death did call them hence a better place to find.

By the path to the east of the churchyard a headstone bears an unusual epitaph which states:

> This Verse was Composed by the Deceased some time before her Death.
> Farewell my dear and loveing Frind
> For here I cannot stay;
> I hope the Lord will be your Guide
> When I am gone hance away
> I hope the Lord will be kind at last
> My suffering will be o'er,
> And I shall be gone up with Christ
> Where sorrows are no more.

MORWENSTOW

The church at Morwenstow in the north-east corner of Cornwall lies in a valley, the cliffs rising to 450 feet on either side. It faces the sea, its tower a landmark to passing ships. A handsome oak lych gate stands at the entrance, flanked by a mortuary shed on one side and a wide slate stile on the other.

This was the parish of poet-Parson Robert Stephen Hawker, vicar of Morwenstow from 1834 to 1875. He built the vicarage below the church, with chimneys imitating two Oxford colleges, three towers of his previous parish churches and his mothers tombstone.

In his book, *Footprints of Former Men in Cornwall*, he describes how he and his parishioners buried between thirty and forty shipwrecked seamen, the crews of three lost vessels, in unmarked graves beneath the trees along the southern side of the churchyard. Nearby the painted figurehead of the *Caledonia* stands over the graves of her crew.

Halfway along the path to the church is a granite chest-tomb to John Manning and his wife Christina. He was killed by a bull in 1601; his wife was so shocked by the tragedy that she died in premature childbirth.

A stone by the porch records the death of Richard Baker, Clerk of this parish for 45 years, who died on the 13th March 1860 aged 75 years; also William Oke, who worked in this church for 50 years. Nearby is the grave of Archdeacon Puddicombe, who slipped on the cliffs and fell to his death in 1904. Also poor William Biss of Taunton 'who was found dead beneath these cliffs on his forty-ninth birthday, October 18th 1875.'

There are some good nineteenth century epitaphs, including one to Richard Seldon who died on 23rd August 1846 'in the 19th year of his Age':

A violent pain did sieze my brain
All in my bloom of days
Death with its dart did pierce my heart
And took my life away.
So quick and sudden was my call
I soon was taken from you all
Death does not always warning give
Therefore be careful how you live.
O haste to God make no delay
For no-one knows his dying day.

Caledonia figurehead, Morwenstow

MYLOR

Mylor churchyard, full of trees and shrubs, slopes down to the quay of the little port. The west entrance has a modern lych gate with a coffin stone. The detached bell tower (1636) with its weatherboarded upper storey is set into the bank with slate headstones pinned to the walls.

The south porch has pretty carved tracery on its outer jambs. Outside stands the Saxon cross, at 17 ft 6 ins the tallest in Cornwall, of which seven feet are in the ground. Traditionally it is said to mark St Mylor's grave.

The churchyard is rich in interesting memorials. The oldest gravestone is the ledger to Thomas Peter, preacher of Mylor 'above 20 years.' who died in 1654 when Cromwell was protector. He was driven from Cornwall by Parliament troops, went out to America and became the first minister of the settlement of New London, returning to Mylor to spend his last years in peace.

A charming epitaph records the sad demise of Joseph Crapp, shipwright, who died ye 26th November 1770:

Alas friend Joseph, His End was All most Sudden
As though the mandate came express

from Heaven
His foot it Slip and he did fall
Help, Help he cries and that was all.
South of the church under the trees is a chest tomb to Wanchope George who died in 1793 aged 60:

Let his errors rest in peace, his excellence deserve admiration, let me with the Wife admire his Wisdom, let the envious and ignorant ridicule his foibles, the folly of others is ever more ridiculous to those who are themselves more foolish.

Nearby is a headstone with great waves and a graphic carving of a ship sinking in a storm:

To the memory of the warriors women and children who on their return to England from the coast of Spain unhappily perished in the wreck of the Queen Transport on Trefusis Point January 14th 1814. This stone is erected as a testimony of regret for their fate by the inhabitants of the parish.

Cross base and shaft, Padstow

PADSTOW

A shaded churchyard with eighteenth century wrought iron gates and a brick and timber lych gate on the east side. Just inside this entrance an early ledger decorated with foliage and flowers is pinned to the wall. It reminds us that this is a seafaring community:

Here lyes the body of Thomas Pearse of this Towne, Mariner, who was buried the fourth day of June anno Domini 1709 aged 54 years.
Tho' Boysterous winds and Billows Sore
Have toss'd me To and Fro
By God's Decree in Spight of both
I rest me here below
When at an Anchor now I lye
With many of our Fleet
One day I shall set Sayl again
Our Saviour for to meet.

A large stone by east gate is an enormous cross-base and part of a shaft, dug up in the churchyard. Langdon says that from the size of it, it would have been the largest cross in Cornwall. Local folklore has it that if anyone should sit on it they would hear the roar of the Devil, incarcerated beneath.

An early slate on the north boundary wall has a winged angel and the erratic spacing of the period. It is in memory of Dorothy Key, late of St Breock, who died in 1678.

The churchyard is full of nineteenth century epitaphs, many of them recording seaside tragedies, including a number of children.

On the north side are five headstones in a row, all to two related families who seem to have had more than their fair share of children lost: William Hutchings, master mariner, and Dorthea (sic) lost Robert aged two years eight months and a brother who died of cholera in E Indies aged 24. Then their son William who was drowned falling over a cliff aged seven. His body was found 23 days later near Bude. Finally they lost a daughter at the age of 27, although William Hutchings, who died in 1897, lived to the ripe old age of 93. Thomas and Mary Deacon lost a son aged five, another son aged three and a son drowned at the age of nineteen. Then their daughter Alberta who died on 28th April 1863 aged 13 mths. Her epitaph is rather engaging:

Dear prattling child to all our hearts most dear
Long shall we bathe thy memory with a tear
Farewell to promising on earth to dwell
Sweetest of fondlings, best of babes farewell.

PAUL

Paul has an ancient cross set into the churchyard walls carved, with the figure of Christ. Near the south-east gate is the obelisk to Dorothy Pentreath which was set up by Prince Loucien Bonaparte. On the stone is the fifth commandment and the claim that she was the last person to speak Cornish. She was reputed to be 102 when she died in 1777, and part of the

Mylor

Memorial to Dolly Pentreath 1777, Paul

inscription is written in Cornish.

The porch has a sundial with Father Time; on the outside wall a slate records the untimely death of three men: John Badcock, John Bryant and John Pearce, three young fishermen, a portion of a little missionary band who left their native land 7th September 1850 on the perilous enterprise of sowing the seeds of Christianity on the barbarous shores of Tierra-del-Fuego and who with their companions there unhappily perished after a series of unparalleled sufferings endured with exemplary fortitude AD 1851.

A slate to Richard Trewavas who died April 13th 1815 has a eulogising epitaph typical of the period:

Nature endow'd him with a manly mind
And Grace his powers illumin'd and refin'd
To be a Christian was his constant aim
And Jesus' love his confidence and theme
The ties of friendship wou'd have held him here
But Heaven design'd him for a brighter sphere.

In the churchyard extension opposite is some pleasing modern work, including a stone to Ann Le Grice carved with a basket of flowers; the slate was taken from the pigsties in her own home.

STRATTON

St Andrew's is a fine hilltop church with gargoyles and pinnacles on the tower and a figure of St Andrew in a niche over the west door. The lychgate was built in the 1930's using oak from the wooden warship *Defiant* in memory of a former incumbent. A slate sundial on the porch overlooks this large and well-maintained churchyard.

On the left of the path is a stone to John Hicks which has an uncommon outline and ribbed marginal decoration. It is by Fanson of Stratton, who describes himself on the stone as 'Engraver.' The inscription reads:

Sacred to the memory of John Hicks, late superannuated Officer of Excise who died at Diddies in this Parish the 12th of July 1823 aged 61 years.
My glass is run my time was come
Death gave the blows and I am gone.
My widow left and children dear
Mourn their loss both far and near.
In God they trust and hope to be
Redeemed by Christ eternally.

To the north of the church is a near life-size bronze figure of a youth playing the harp. It marks the grave of Anca Winand van Wulfften Palthe who died in 1922, and is by T. Rosandic.

An enigmatic epitaph records the death of William Bickford who died on February 1st 1809 aged 50.

Honest men we seldom meet
Here lies one beneath your feet.
Let it to the world be known,
Thou art one who reads this stone.

Unusual shape and decorative edging 1823, Stratton

Harping youth in bronze 1922, Stratton

ST STEPHEN-BY-SALTASH

St Stephen's is a large, raised churchyard, the slate headstones laid out in regimented rows. A number of headstones have relief carvings of angels or chest tombs with classical weepers and drooping sheaves of foliage.

There are several memorials to the Screech family, evidently a local name:

Charles Screech was unfortunately drowned in coming up Hamoaze on Thursday evening April 10th 1834, was found the 6th of May and interred the subsequent day aged 62 years:

All you that come my grave to see
Prepare yourselves to follow me
Repent with speed, make no delay
For I in haste was called away
Weep not for me my wife most kind
Nor you my children left behind
Death does not always warning give
Therefore be careful how you live.
I left my wife and children dear
They little thought my time so near
But may we meet in Heaven and be

Happy throughout eternity.

A vivid epitaph records the travels of Theobald Butler, 'late of the City of Dublin in Ireland and late Gunner of the Ocean' who died at Saltash the 18th day of June 1782 aged 56 years.

For forty years I plow'd the raging Main
Through Europe, Africa and back again
Thence to America, touched Asia too
Yet here I rest, reader, waiting for you,
Careless of storms, or tempest or cannon loudly roaring
As here I lie I now defy all officers controling
Tho in my life I did discharge my duty with delight
Never more eas'd nor better pleased my enemy to fight.

There is a rare stone with an unusual dedication:

This stone is erected by the noncommissioned officers and men of the Plymouth division of the Royal Marines in memory of Mary May who died the 2nd October 1860 aged 76 years. Also of her mother Mary Blake who died the 7th June 1841 aged 40 years. The mother and daughter supplied the Royal Marine barracks at Stonehouse with shellfish for more than half a century and gained the good opinion of all their customers by their sterling honesty and kind and unassuming demeanour.

ST TEATH

The churchyard at St Teath is large and pleasantly uncut, with celandines and crocuses growing wild; one determined gentleman persisted in mowing a single plot with a hand mower. The church room which forms part of the boundary is now a community centre.

There are some good eighteenth century stones with angels and skulls attached to the east wall of the church. Several headstones in the churchyard have a particular embellishment to the first letter of the word 'Here' which seems to be a feature of a local craftsman.

Headstones in regimented lines, Saltash

A stone with an angel records the death of the two small children of John and Margaret Trayes in 1774:

> Beneath this Stone Two Sweet Babes here doth lie
> Not Lost, but rest until the riseing day;
> They shall with Saints and Angels joyfull pass
> Such endless Joy as no Tongue can Express.

A draped urn decorates the stone to Hugh Lukey 'who was accidently kill'd at Delabole Quarry on the 23rd of July 1844 at the age of 27.' The epitaph describes the shock of the bereaved:

> Our friend in the morning in health might be seen
> The Lord thought it fit it was wither'd at noon.
> How short was the warning, how sudden the call
> To friends how alarming, it was awful to all.

A similar fate seems to have befallen George Harry, 'who was suddenly launch'd into Eternity' on February 6th 1843 at the age of 24.

> O reader now who e'er you be
> That read these lines concerning me;
> How God can quickly stop your breath
> Prepare! Prepare for sudden Death.

Decorative lettering 1765, St Teath

FURTHER READING

Bizley, A. C. **The Slate Figures of Cornwall**. 1965
Burgess, F. **English Churchyard Memorials.** Lutterworth Press,1963
Child, M. **Discovering Churchyards.** Shire Publications,1989
Johnson, N. & Rose, P. **Cornwall's Archaeological Heritage.** Twelveheads Press,1990
Langdon, A. G. **Old Cornish Crosses.** 1896
Lindley, K. **Of Graves and Epitaphs.** Hutchinson,1965
Mee, A. **Cornwall.** Hodder & Stoughton, 1937
Saunders, A. **Devon & Cornwall.** HMSO, 1991

USEFUL ADDRESSES

Church and Conservation Project, The Arthur Rank Centre, National Agricultural Centre, Stoneleigh, Warwickshire CV8 2LZ. Tel: 01203 696969
Cornwall Family History Society, 5 Victoria Square, Truro TR1 2RS
Cornwall Wildlife Trust, Five Acres, Allet, Truro TR4 9DJ Tel: 01872 73939
Royal Commission on Historical Monuments of England, Kemsle Drive, Swindon SN2 2GZ Tel: 01793 414600
Memorials by Artists, Snape Priory, Saxmundham, Suffolk IP17 1SA Tel: 01728 688934

ACKNOWLEDGMENTS
Excerpt from *Churchyards* by John Betjeman reproduced by kind permission of John Murray.
Illustration from *The Slate Figures of Cornwall* reproduced by kind permission of Alice C Bizley.

3463